Y0-AQV-638

Mama Says . . .
Don't Drive
Faster Than
Your Guardian
Angel Can Fly

Visit Tyndale's exciting Web site at www.tyndale.com

Edited by Lisa A. Jackson

Designed by Beth Sparkman

ISBN 0-8423-5191-4

Printed in China

06   05   04   03   02
5   4   3   2   1

Don't Drive Faster Than Your Guardian Angel Can Fly

Rita J. Maggart

TYNDALE

Tyndale House Publishers, Inc.
Wheaton, Illinois

Dedicated to
Mother and Memama

Acknowledgments

The gestation of *Mama Says* began with a casual conversation with an acquaintance at my church about my need for help with the promotion of my first book, *In the Growing Places*. She suggested that I call Amy Lyles Wilson, then an editor with a publishing house in Nashville. Amy and I met and she sent me to Sabrina Cashwell, a book publicist. Sabrina led me to Evergreen Ideas and the book and product development team of Andy Hyde and Debbie Bush. Andy and Debbie presented my ideas to many publishers. We were excited when Tyndale House Publishers came to Nashville and gave us an interview. Andy and Debbie believed in my ability, and Tyndale House saw the potential of *Mama Says* as a way to communicate with Christian parents.

After contract negotiations with my attorney, Derek Crownover, and with my agreement in hand, I could then return to Amy Lyles Wilson and say, "Let's get to work!" With her guidance and the expert computer skills of Mary MacKinnon, the manuscript began to develop. The give-and-take of Tyndale House editors Karen Watson and Lisa Jackson and art director Beth Sparkman, along with the skill of artist Luke Daab, proved to be a blending of talented business professionals to develop a quality book.

These people have given this book life outside of my home. But *Mama Says* was conceived inside my home as I searched for better ways to communicate with my children. Thanks to my husband, John, and our three sons, Brad, Bill, and Stephen, I was given a reason to grow and mature as a wife and mother. My mother, grandmothers, and mother-in-law knew it would take all the mothers I could get to raise these three boys to manhood, and so we nurtured them together.

The birthing of this book has taken business professionals, friends, and family members, and it hasn't happened overnight. The fine art of mothering doesn't happen overnight either. For me, it began with the birth of my first child in 1974 and will continue for the rest of my life. Sharing what's inside my heart is my job, and remember, it's your job, too.

Rita J. Maggart

*Throughout this book
you'll see the symbol · O ·.
This is a secret we use in our family
to send the message* I Love You.

Dear friends,

The most humbling job in the world is parenting. And it's not made easier when your child becomes a teenager! My mother always told me, "Tell your children what they need to hear; that's the best you can do." *Mama Says . . . Don't Drive Faster Than Your Guardian Angel Can Fly* is another opportunity for you to do just that.

Teens are continuously asking these questions: "How do I look?" "Does anybody like me?" "Why am I here?"

When you stop to think about it, these are the same questions adults ask. We just pretend to know the answers. Teenagers are always searching and crying out for the guidance of godly parents and teachers. As parents, we often provide the "stuff and run" kind of communication for our teenagers, when what they really need is "heart to heart." This is why it's important for us to make our words count.

We must craft our words into meaning. Our children can't be ready for an exam unless they've studied, and the same is true for us. We parents can't be ready to give good advice unless we've done our own homework of Bible study, prayer, and example-setting. Even though our teens might wish at times that they could make it without us, they really do need their parents.

When we were given the gifts of these precious children, we were also given a huge job—the most humbling job in the world.

I hope this *Mama Says* book will help to jump-start your own words to your own child. Think of it as a workbook for you to jot down your thoughts, quotes, and inspirations. In the back you'll find instructions for writing your own personal *Mama Says*.

Remember, we're all in this together.

Your friend,
Rita J. Maggart

There will come a day when the *more* clothes
you put on the better you look.

· O ·

Charm is deceptive, and beauty does not last;
but a woman who fears the Lord will be greatly praised.
PROVERBS 31:30

Sex outside of marriage
always hurts somebody.

· O ·

The man who commits adultery is an utter fool,
for he destroys his own soul.
PROVERBS 6:32

Mama Says...

Begin today

to win tomorrow.

· O ·

The end of a matter is better than its beginning.
ECCLESIASTES 7:8, NASB

Get off the computer and get into a book.

· O ·

Do you understand what you are reading?
ACTS 8:30

Your daily life says more about you
than what you wear.

· O ·

Whatever you do or say, let it be as a
representative of the Lord Jesus.
COLOSSIANS 3:17

Look deeper than someone's appearance.

· O ·

Don't be concerned about the outward beauty that
depends on fancy hairstyles, expensive jewelry,
or beautiful clothes.

1 PETER 3:3

Make time to make art.

· O ·

The desire accomplished is sweet to the soul.
PROVERBS 13:19, KJV

Perseverance is the No. 1 key to success.

· O ·

I suggest that you finish what you started a year
ago. . . . You should carry this project through
to completion just as enthusiastically as you began it.

2 CORINTHIANS 8:10-11

When you think about doing something
stupid, think about the people who love you.

· O ·

It is painful to be the parent of a fool.
PROVERBS 17:21

Be nice.

· O ·

Do for others what you would like them to do for you.
MATTHEW 7:12

Never lie,

cheat,

or steal.

In each case you hurt someone else.

· O ·

A good man hates lies.
PROVERBS 13:5, TLB

If you cheat even a little, you won't be
honest with greater responsibilities.
LUKE 16:10

Thou shalt not steal.
EXODUS 20:15, KJV

You are known by the company you keep.

· O ·

Bad company corrupts good character.
1 CORINTHIANS 15:33

Be careful.

· O ·

You . . . belong to God; so run from all these evil things,
and follow what is right and good.

1 TIMOTHY 6:11

Either do it or don't do it,
but don't complain about it.

· O ·

In everything you do, stay away from
complaining and arguing.
PHILIPPIANS 2:14

Mama Says...

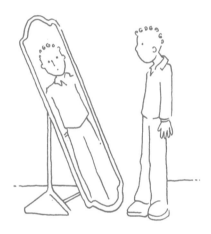

The only person you can change is yourself.

· O ·

Be made new in the attitude of your minds.
EPHESIANS 4:23, NIV

Pretty is as pretty does.

· O ·

You should be known for the beauty
that comes from within, the unfading beauty of a
gentle and quiet spirit, which is so precious to God.
1 PETER 3:4

Mama Says...

Conflict, rejection, and unhappiness can give
you new resolve and make you stronger,
but you must *choose* that reaction.

· O ·

Choose today whom you will serve.
JOSHUA 24:15

The richest people are content with little.

· O ·

I have learned how to get along happily
whether I have much or little.
PHILIPPIANS 4:11

There's a big difference between what
you need and what you want.

· O ·

And even when you do ask, you don't get it
because your whole motive is wrong—you want
only what wiii give you pleasure.

JAMES 4:3

God has picked you out to be his own.

· O ·

I have called you by name; you are mine.
ISAIAH 43:1

Mama Says...

Look for the
challenge.

Remember that in a race everyone runs, but only one person
gets the prize. You also must run in such a way that you will
win. All athletes practice strict self-control. They do it to win a
prize that will fade away, but we do it for an eternal prize.

1 CORINTHIANS 9:24–25

You can learn a lot from the people
you don't agree with.

· O ·

We are perplexed, but we don't give up and quit.
2 CORINTHIANS 4:8

Mama Says...

Godly adults can help you
make decisions. Just ask.

· O ·

The godly offer good counsel;
they know what is right from wrong.
PSALM 37:30

God sees your tears and hears your cries.

· O ·

Jesus said, "Come to me, all of you who are weary and
carry heavy burdens, and I will give you rest."
MATTHEW 11:28

Look carefully at your girlfriend's mother—
that's who she'll be in 20 years.

· O ·

Like mother, like daughter.
EZEKIEL 16:44

Don't drink and drive.

· O ·

Think soberly.
ROMANS 12:3, KJV

Mama Says...

Don't drive faster than your
guardian angel can fly.

· O ·

The wise are cautious and avoid danger;
fools plunge ahead with great confidence.
PROVERBS 14:16

What *would* Jesus do?

· O ·

I have given you an example to follow.
Do as I have done to you.
JOHN 13:15

Mama Says. . .

Your eyes are the windows to your soul.

· O ·

Your eye is a lamp for your body. A pure eye lets
sunshine into your soul. But an evil eye shuts out
the light and plunges you into darkness.

LUKE 11:34

Write a note. Encourage a friend.
The kindness you show will
return to you again.

· O ·

If you give, you will receive. Your gift will return to you in full
measure, pressed down, shaken together to make room for
more, and running over.

LUKE 6:38

When you're in bad company, leave.

· O ·

Watch out for people who cause divisions and upset
people's faith by teaching things that are contrary to
what you have been taught. Stay away from them.
Such people are not serving Christ our Lord; they
are serving their own personal interests.

ROMANS 16:17-18

It takes a million moments of input for
one golden moment of output.

Read, read, read
Study, study, study
Think, think, think
Learn, learn, learn
Share, share, share
Practice, practice, practice

· O ·

Work hard so God can approve you.
2 TIMOTHY 2:15

Mama Says...

Don't leave home without saying good-bye.

· O ·

Finally, brothers, good-by. Aim for perfection, listen
to my appeal, be of one mind, live in peace. And the
God of love and peace will be with you.

2 CORINTHIANS 13:11, NIV

If you're truly sorry, you won't do it again.

· O ·

Confess your sin to the LORD, the God of your
ancestors, and do what he demands.
EZRA 10:11

Mama Says...

If your friend jumps
off a cliff
are you going to
jump too?

· O ·

YAAAAAAAA

Don't copy the behavior and customs of this world,
but let God transform you into a new person
by changing the way you think.

ROMANS 12:2

Don't be afraid to fail.
Do be afraid of not living
up to your potential.

· O ·

I am holding you by your right hand—I, the LORD your God.
And I say to you, "Do not be afraid. I am here to help you."

ISAIAH 41:13

Good friends make you better;
bad friends don't.

· O ·

As iron sharpens iron, a friend sharpens a friend.
PROVERBS 27:17

Let it go. Holding a grudge stifles your productivity.

Come to terms quickly with your enemy before
it is too late and you are dragged into court.

MATTHEW 5:25

Mama Says...

Wishing for someone to be nice to you will never make it happen. You must be nice first.

· O ·

Do for others what you would like them to do for you.
MATTHEW 7:12

You've got to know where you're going
before you can get there.

· O ·

Look! He has placed it in front of you. Go and occupy
it as the LORD, the God of your ancestors, has promised you.
Don't be afraid! Don't be discouraged!

DEUTERONOMY 1:21

Mama Says...

You're here for a purpose.

· O ·

All who claim me as their God will come, for I have made
them for my glory. It was I who created them.
ISAIAH 43:7

God has big plans for you. Are you listening?

· O ·

I knew you before I formed you in your mother's womb.
Before you were born I set you apart and appointed
you as my spokesman to the world.

JEREMIAH 1:4-5

Real men *do* cry.

· O ·

Jesus wept.
JOHN 11:35, KJV

Every person has
a gift from God.
What is yours?

· O ·

All must give as they are able, according to the
blessings given to them by the LORD your God.
DEUTERONOMY 16:17

Mama Says...

Stay in the growing places.

· O ·

I am holding you by your right hand—I, the LORD your God.
And I say to you, "Do not be afraid. I am here to help you."
ISAIAH 41:13

Be an original.

· O ·

God has given each of us the ability to do certain things well.
ROMANS 12:6

Mama Says...

Look for ways to volunteer.

· O ·

Strengthen those who have tired hands,
and encourage those who have weak knees.
ISAIAH 35:3

Rejoice and let the spirit move you.

· O ·

The Spirit of the LORD came upon Gideon,
and he blew a trumpet.

JUDGES 6:34, KJV

Mama Says...

Pay attention when unexpected people
enter your life; they may be
miracles about to happen.

· O ·

Don't forget to show hospitality to strangers, for some who
have done this have entertained angels without realizing it!
HEBREWS 13:2

Never give up hope.

· O ·

When dreams come true at last, there is life and joy.
PROVERBS 13:12, TLB

Mama Says...

Hope is your doctor's best friend
and your own best medicine.

· O ·

She thought, "If I can just touch his robe, I will be healed."
MATTHEW 9:21

When you do the "right" thing,
you'll know it.

· O ·

Songs of joy and victory are sung in the camp of the godly.
PSALM 118:15

Mama Says...

Love is a dance of give and take.

· O ·

Love does not demand its own way.
1 CORINTHIANS 13:5

Jealousy shows
in your speech,
in your face, and
in your body language,
and it doesn't make you pretty.

· O ·

You are jealous for what others have, and you can't possess
it, so you fight and quarrel to take it away from them.
JAMES 4:2

Mama Says...

True love is loyalty to the end.

· O ·

Love never gives up, never loses faith, is always hopeful,
and endures through every circumstance.
1 CORINTHIANS 13:7

One act of love is worth more than
a million words of love.

· O ·

Dear children, let us stop just saying we love each other;
let us really show it by our actions.
1 JOHN 3:18

HM,
HM,
HMMM...

You can't listen when you're speaking, and
you can't learn when you're not listening.

· O ·

Listen and learn quietly.
1 TIMOTHY 2:11

Hug your mama—you might be
surprised at the results!

· O ·

If we love each other, God lives in us, and his love
has been brought to full expression through us.
1 JOHN 4:12

If you're tuned in to God you'll know
who you're supposed to help,
when you're supposed to help,
and
how you're supposed to help.

· O ·

Work at bringing others to Christ.
Complete the ministry God has given you.
2 TIMOTHY 4:5

Study with a mentor until you can work on
your own with confidence.

· O ·

Whoso loveth instruction loveth knowledge:
but he that hateth reproof is brutish.
PROVERBS 12:1, KJV

Mama Says...

Don't begin the day until you've prayed.

· O ·

Listen to my voice in the morning, LORD. Each morning
I bring my requests to you and wait expectantly.
PSALM 5:3

Pray for God's help in choosing
a wife or husband.

· O ·

Parents can provide their sons with an inheritance of houses
and wealth, but only the LORD can give an understanding wife.
PROVERBS 19:14

Mama Says...

Get up and try again.

· O ·

We get knocked down, but we get up again and keep going.
2 CORINTHIANS 4:9

Say to someone else what *you* need to hear
and you'll both feel better.

· O ·

Good people enjoy the positive results of their words.
PROVERBS 13:2

Mama Says...

Serve your country
and it will serve you back.

· O ·

Surely this great nation is a wise and understanding people.
DEUTERONOMY 4:6, KJV

Face your problems first.
Everything else will seem easy.

· O ·

Don't try to squirm out of your problems.
JAMES 1:4, TLB

Mama Says...

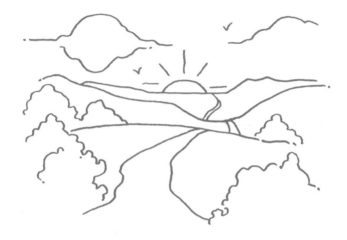

Your day is coming.

· O ·

These things I plan won't happen right away.
Slowly, steadily, surely, the time approaches when the
vision will be fulfilled. If it seems slow, wait patiently,
for it will surely take place. It will not be delayed.
HABAKKUK 2:3

Take responsibility for your own actions.

· O ·

Brace yourself, because I have some questions for you,
and you must answer them.

JOB 38:3

Show respect to people who are older than you, and you'll earn respect in return.

· O ·

Show your fear of God by standing up in the presence
of elderly people and showing respect for the aged.
I am the LORD.
LEVITICUS 19:32

Pick up after yourself.

· O ·

Each one should carry his own load.
GALATIANS 6:5, NIV

When you think nobody cares about you,
remember—God does.

· O ·

Give all your worries and cares to God,
for he cares about what happens to you.
1 PETER 5:7

Don't smoke. It makes you smell bad.

· O ·

Instead of smelling of sweet perfume, they will stink.
ISAIAH 3:24

If you play with fire,
you're going to get burned.

· O ·

Can a man scoop fire into his lap and not be burned?
PROVERBS 6:27

Your mouth is your own best friend
or your own worst enemy.

· O ·

The mouths of fools are their ruin;
their lips get them into trouble.
PROVERBS 18:7

Mama Says...

You are sweeter than honey,
so says your mother.

· O ·

Sweeter also than honey and the honeycomb.
PSALM 19:10, KJV

Sometimes, the less you say,
the smarter you sound.

· O ·

Being a fool makes you a blabbermouth.
ECCLESIASTES 5:3, TLB

The busyness of the day is filled with
interruptions. So, get up early or stay up late.
Otherwise you've sealed your fate.

· O ·

Whatever you do, do well. For when you go to the grave,
there will be no work or planning or knowledge or wisdom.
ECCLESIASTES 9:10

If you can't say anything nice,
don't say anything at all.

· O ·

The tongue is a small thing, but what enormous damage it
can do. A tiny spark can set a great forest on fire.

JAMES 3:5

Keep a mirror near your telephone
so you can *see* how you sound.

· O ·

As a face is reflected in water,
so the heart reflects the person.
PROVERBS 27:19

Love your brothers and sisters.

· O ·

How wonderful it is, how pleasant, when
brothers live together in harmony!
PSALM 133:1

Mama Says...

In silence answers are found.
In silence peace is felt.
In silence creativity is sparked.
In silence energy is renewed.
In silence thoughts are released.
In silence the mind is cleared.
In silence gentleness is restored.
In silence self-worth is established.
In silence the body is healed.
In silence the hearing is keened.
In silence I talk with God.
In silence I am one with myself.

· O ·

Be silent, and know that I am God!
PSALM 46:10

False teachers will tickle your ears.

· O ·

A time is coming when people will no longer listen to right teaching. They will follow their own desires and will look for teachers who will tell them whatever they want to hear. They will reject the truth and follow strange myths.

2 TIMOTHY 4:3-4

Mama Says...

Write thank-you notes
to your ministers and teachers.

· O ·

Honor those who are your leaders in the Lord's work.
1 THESSALONIANS 5:12

If you want to learn something, teach it.

· O ·

If you teach others, why don't you teach yourself?
ROMANS 2:21

Mama Says...

What a person thinks about
is what a person talks about.

· O ·

Fix your thoughts on what is true and honorable and right.
Think about things that are pure and lovely and admirable.
Think about things that are excellent and worthy of praise.

PHILIPPIANS 4:8

Clean out the inside
before dressing up
the outside.

· O ·

It is the thought-life that defiles you. For from within,
out of a person's heart, come evil thoughts, sexual immorality,
theft, murder, adultery, greed, wickedness, deceit, eagerness
for lustful pleasure, envy, slander, pride, and foolishness.
All these vile things come from within; they are what
defile you and make you unacceptable to God.

MARK 7:20-23

Surround yourself with honest people.

· O ·

Find some capable, honest men who fear God
and hate bribes. . . . They will help you carry the load,
making the task easier for you.
EXODUS 18:21-22

Do what you do well, and do it for God.

· O ·

Work hard and cheerfully at whatever you do, as though you
were working for the Lord rather than for people.

COLOSSIANS 3:23

Mama Says...

Remember, I will always love you!

· O ·

I close my letter with these last words: Be happy. Grow in Christ. Pay attention to what I have said. Live in harmony and peace. And may the God of love and peace be with you.

2 CORINTHIANS 13:11, TLB

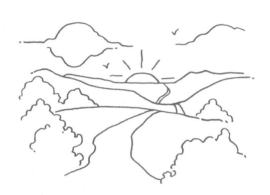

The best book you'll ever read will be the one you write yourself. Now it's your turn. What you have to say to your child is really what's important. The real value of this "Mama Says" book is to stimulate your own thinking. And the notes you've made in this book could be the beginning of a new method of communicating with your child. Every moment you spend in reading, writing, or researching with your child as the focus of your attention will be time well spent. You'll have two gifts: a tangible book and the opportunity to become a new and better mother as you develop your own relationship with God through listening and discernment as God speaks to you. What more could a child ask for?

Here is my recipe for writing a "Mama Says" book. You will develop and refine your own method, but for now, these are my suggestions on how to begin.

One more thing: don't be offended if your handiwork is not read immediately. Someday, when the child is ready, he or she will appreciate your efforts. For today, be satisfied with your own best effort, and remember . . .

"Tell your children what they need to hear. That's the best you can do."

Train up a child in the way he should go:
and when he is old, he will not depart from it.
PROVERBS 22:6, KJV

Materials

- Inspirational reading material
- Pencil and paper (a junior legal pad is my favorite)
- Blank book (I like a spiral-bound book so I can make changes easily.)
- Resource books
- Computer (optional) to input your material—but when I'm reading, I use a pencil and paper to take notes.

Method

- Find a time and place conducive to reading and writing—this is the hardest part.
- Read until you're ready to write. God will speak to you as you read.
- Jot down thoughts and reflections while reading or whenever you remember things your mother, grandmother, aunt, and mentors said.
- Free-associate. You can organize your scribbles later.
- Keep your notes. You may want to develop a filing system or computer program for this information.
- Transfer (rewrite) your notes into a blank book. Personalize with photos, stencils, cutouts, drawings—anything that makes an inviting book for your child.
- Use a topical resource book for help with Scripture references and a quotation resource book for famous quotations.

- Give each page a theme (or subject).
- Give yourself plenty of time. For example, set a goal of one year or for a graduation, wedding, birthday, or Christmas gift. This is an ongoing project, so revel in the process.
- Enjoy your time alone with God as you partner in communication with your child. Mother Teresa said, "I am just a little pencil, the work is God's work" (*A Gift for God*).

Favorite Resource Books

- *The Complete Book of Bible Quotations*
- *The Handbook of Bible Application*
- *The New Strong's Exhaustive Concordance*
- *Today's Parallel Bible*; New International Version, Updated Edition; *New American Standard Bible*; King James Version; New Living Translation
- *The TouchPoint Bible*
- Feel free to use any quotations from this book!

Favorite Inspirational Reading

- *Adventure in Prayer*, Catherine Marshall
- *Becoming a Woman of Influence*, Carol Kent
- *Beyond Ourselves*, Catherine Marshall
- *The Burden Is Light*, Eugenia Price
- *A Closer Walk*, Catherine Marshall
- *Disciplines of a Beautiful Woman*, Anne Ortland
- *The Friendship Factor*, Alan Loy McGinnis
- *The Fruit of the Spirit*, Sarah Hornsby

- *A Gift for God*, Mother Teresa
- *The Helper*, Catherine Marshall
- *How to Keep a Spiritual Journal*, Ronald Klug
- *Lord, Change Me*, Evelyn Christenson
- *Make Love Your Aim*, Eugenia Price
- *Mr. Jones, Meet the Master*, Catherine Marshall
- *Speak Up with Confidence*, Carol Kent
- *Something Beautiful for God*, Malcolm Muggeridge
- *Soul Feast*, Marjorie Thompson
- *Walking on Water*, Madeleine L'Engle
- *Woman to Woman*, Eugenia Price

For information on scheduling Rita Maggart to speak for your event, please contact Speak Up Speaker Services toll free at (888) 870-7719 or email: speakupinc@aol.com

Mama Says...

Mama Says...

Mama Says...

Mama Says...

Mama Says...

Mama Says...

Mama Says . . . You Can Always
Come Home for Advice
Kitchen table wisdom from the heart

Mama Says . . . Don't Drive Faster
Than Your Guardian Angel Can Fly
A care package from home

Mama Says . . . Cookies Cure a
Lot of Things
Encouragement for new parents